Acknowledgements
Many thanks to the following photographers whose remarkable
work is represented in these pages:

David LaChapelle
Richard Pereira/Art Direction by Terry O'Neill
Gavin Bond
David Appleby
Nick Wall

The publisher would also like to thank the following people for
their invaluable assistance with this book:

At Rocket Pictures: David Furnish and Rachael Paley

At MARV Films: Emily Castel

At Paramount Pictures:
　Worldwide Photography:
Holly Connors
Denise Cubbins
　Production:
Jon Gonda
Steven Jackson
　Licensing:
Kevin Suh
Adele Plumail
Risa Kessler
Sabi Lofgren

Photo credit
Page 160 Michael Kovac/Getty Images for EJAF.

weldon**owen**

Published in North America by
Weldon Owen International
1045 Sansome Street
San Francisco, CA 94111
www.weldonowen.com

President & Publisher: Roger Shaw
Associate Publisher: Mariah Bear

First published in the UK in 2019 by Carlton Books Limited

Editorial Director: Roland Hall
Design: Russell Knowles
Production: Rachel Burgess
Text: Malcolm Croft

Library of Congress Cataloging in Publication data is available.

ISBN: 978-1-68188-479-0

10 9 8 7 6 5 4 3 2 1

Printed in Canada

INSIDE THE WORLD OF THE MOVIE

FOREWORD BY
ELTON JOHN

weldon**owen**

★ CONTENTS

FOREWORD
BY ELTON JOHN
6

CHAPTER 1
SCRIPT TO SCREEN
8

CHAPTER 2
BECOMING ELTON
14

CHAPTER 3
SHOOTING STARS
28

CHAPTER 4
THIS IS MY SONG
48

CHAPTER 5
THE WORLD'S A STAGE
84

CHAPTER 6
THE SHY BOY FROM PINNER
102

CHAPTER 7
FROM LONDON TO L.A.
116

CHAPTER 8
FOR MY NEXT TRICK
134

CHAPTER 9
**THE BIGGEST PLATFORM
BOOTS KNOWN TO MAN**
144

★

FOREWORD
BY ELTON JOHN

If producing a musical fantasy based on your own life seems surreal to you, trust me, it feels beyond surreal to me. Never did I think that I would be fortunate enough to see this ambitious project come to life, let alone see it made by such a talented team of filmmakers and creatives, many of whom I am blessed to now call my good friends. It's been a magical experience, albeit one during which I have wondered, on more than a few occasions, "How on earth are we going to pull this off?" I have no idea how everyone kept sane.

Of course, it is the shared vision of Dexter Fletcher, David Furnish, Matthew Vaughn, Adam Bohling, David Reid and Lee Hall who have made all of this possible. I am forever grateful for the blood, sweat and tears that they have given to this project for me. I'd also like to extend my gratitude to all the fabulous actors who have brought to life the people who helped shape mine, and to Taron, in particular, who appears in every bloody scene. For you to become me every day must have been a massive strain, but the fact that you appeared to do it with such grace and enthusiasm… well, it's little wonder that the whole production team is in awe of your talent and commitment.

And, of course, to everyone involved with the production, the legendary Music Producer Giles Martin, the cinematographer George Richmond, the editor Chris Dickens, assistant directors, the production and set designers, the dancers, the location managers, make-up artists and Julian Day, our incredible costume designer – thank you. You have all reminded me how lucky I am for the life I have lived. It's been a wild ride, for sure.
I wonder what's next?

★ CHAPTER 1: **SCRIPT TO SCREEN**

★

SCRIPT TO SCREEN

The journey of Elton's life from script to screen has been a case of art imitating life since the project was first announced in September 2011. After several stop-starts, *Rocketman* finally took flight in front of the camera in August 2018, with acclaimed *Sunshine on Leith* and *Eddie the Eagle* director, Dexter Fletcher. But for the film's writer, award-winning playwright Lee Hall, coaxing Elton John's story to life on the page was more than just a regular job – it felt almost like fate.

"I've been working on it with Elton for a long time," Hall said of the script on the BBC in 2014. "It's an absolutely huge, crazy technicolor affair."

Rocketman is Hall and Elton's second collaboration following the Tony award-winning boy-who-does-ballet film drama *Billy Elliot* (directed by Stephen Daldry, 2000), adapted from Hall's West End play, *Dancer*.

"The more I talked to Elton, the more I realized that he *was* Billy Elliot," Hall explained. "He went to the Royal Academy when he was about 13 and he was studying to be a classical pianist and he discovered Elvis Presley and the rest is history."

Labelling *Rocketman* as "a sequel, in a way," to *Billy Elliot*, Hall felt close to this legendary lead character, allowing him an intimate and unique perspective on the motivations and insecurities of Elton. The fact that Elton knew and trusted Hall and gave him "incredible free rein" on the script ("Elton's never commented once on the script, he hasn't interfered at all,") also allowed the writer to indulge in flamboyant flights of fancy for the film's spectacular set pieces, something any other screenwriter may not have dared, or had permission, to do. "It's all-singing, all-dancing," Hall would aptly summarize of the first draft of his script.

"I WAS BLOWN AWAY BY HOW MAD THE SCRIPT WAS."

RICHARD MADDEN

"*Rocketman* will be a radically different kind of biopic," one of the film's Executive Producers Steve Hamilton Shaw first revealed in 2011. "It will be as unique as Elton's life, told in a non-linear and hyper-visual manner that will transport people through the many intense experiences, some wonderful, some not, that helped define Elton as an artist, musician and man." The producers have never wavered from this vision, despite its challenges.

In April 2018, after more than five years of Hall honing his script, Dexter Fletcher was confirmed as the director of the project, though the movie-maker had been working on the film behind the scenes with producer Matthew Vaughn before cameras rolled.

"I've been attached for two years," explained Fletcher. "I heard that Matthew Vaughn, who's an old mate, and who produced *Eddie the Eagle* with Taron [Egerton] and I, was involved. Matthew just started talking to me like I was doing it, which is his way, he's very smart. And I wasn't smart enough to just ignore that, and just said, 'yeah, exactly.'"

As always, it was the power and pull of Hall's script that sparked Fletcher's imagination. "It was when I read the Lee Hall script that I understood that, here was a film that opened with a man sitting down in rehab saying, 'I'm an alcoholic, and a cocaine addict, and a bulimic.' Immediately I was like, OK, here's a list of seven really dark processes and parts of the human psyche of someone that we think we know, that are going to be unpacked throughout this story. That's what got me engaged."

Opposite Behind the scenes, director Dexter Fletcher consults with producers Elton John and David Furnish on the film's complex set designs.

Above Fletcher, Furnish and Elton discuss the Parklands Hospital set design using 3D card models.

Right Producer Matthew Vaughn and director Dexter Fletcher on set.

Opposite Above Elton discusses all the fun of the fairground scene.

Opposite Below Marcus Rowland, Production Designer: "From that card model, we can pull the scene apart and decide where we need more space for the choreography and where the lights will be."

★ CHAPTER 2: **BECOMING ELTON**

★

BECOMING ELTON

With Taron Egerton, *Rocketman* has the perfect Elton John. One look at the 29-year-old actor as Elton and it's hard to think of anyone else who could step into the singer's legendary shoes – and six-inch platform boots – any better.

Egerton was announced as Elton in April 2018, after a list of young actors had been attached to the role since 2011, including Tom Hardy and Justin Timberlake. Again, as with Hall's appointment as scriptwriter, Egerton's landing of the role feels rather serendipitous.

"The conversation started when we were filming *Kingsman: The Golden Circle* in 2016," Egerton told Radio X. "And I just put my cards on the table and said I was desperate to do it."

It wouldn't be long before Egerton would get the thumbs-up from Elton John and the producers at Rocket Pictures, Elton's and David Furnish's film production company. Unexpectedly, it was his singing as Johnny the gorilla in 2016's *Sing* that would eventually become his audition. "I think when Elton heard *I'm Still Standing*, that kind of sealed the deal," he revealed.

Before Egerton began transforming himself for the role, the actor visited David and Elton at home, where the singer gave him access to his 1970s diaries (never before published), as well as taking Egerton aside and sharing three words of wisdom – "Don't copy me."

Egerton took the advice as gospel. "What I've tried to do is to capture the spirit of him, rather than do an impersonation of him; it's my take on him," he said. "I'm scared everyone's going to hate it!"

Egerton should have no reason to panic. His cast and crewmates are astounded by his portrayal of the icon. If Elton John is a role of a lifetime, then Egerton (like Elton at Dodger Stadium) knocks it way out of the park.

"Taron looks the part, sounds the part, sings the part, *is* the part," explained Tom Bennett, who plays Fred Farebrother, Elton's adored stepfather. "I had whole days where I would just watch Taron on the monitor, just plink-plonking out *Your Song*. He might have done it 47 times, but every time he did it, it was magical and beautiful and brought a tear to people's eyes."

"I always thought that was a brilliant idea to have Taron play Elton," said Fletcher of his leading man. "Taron has this very likeable, vulnerable quality, that not a lot of actors easily find. He has an incredible range. But to be able to step up into this world, for him I think, is something that was really exciting too. When you've got an actor like Taron, who's so engaged, when he's given the opportunity to do something where he's allowed to snot and dribble and sweat and scream and shout and then sing a song – then he doesn't hold back."

One of the biggest challenges for Lizzie Georgiou, Hair and Makeup Designer, and her team was getting Elton's teeth into Taron's mouth. "When I first read the script and started to look at the photographs of Elton, the gap in his teeth was the first thing that kind of came to my mind," she said. "Taron's got these lovely straight beautiful white teeth, and obviously Elton's teeth are very different to that. So we did have to work on some teeth. First of all, we made a little see-through mouth guard that actually fitted in and gave him those little gaps in the teeth. But then Dexter was really worried that Taron might lisp a little bit. Taron was desperate to keep the gaps, because he felt that was part of the character. So, in the end, we painted the gaps in! I've got this special tattoo ink especially for teeth. It looks like the teeth are not straight, but it's actually just a little bit of paint!"

Opposite Taron Egerton as young Elton.

"THERE'S SO MANY TIMES WHERE I'VE BEEN AT THE MONITOR WATCHING WHAT TARON IS DOING, AND HAVE JUST LOOKED AT DEXTER AND SAID 'GOD, HE'S GOOD, ISN'T HE?' YOU KNOW. HE'S REALLY GOOD. AND DEXTER'S LIKE 'I KNOW.'" JAMIE BELL

MAKING UP THE MAN

Lizzie Georgiou, *Rocketman*'s make-up guru, reveals how Taron Egerton transformed into Elton John…every single day.

"When I first came on board Dexter had already talked Taron through what the make-up element of the film entailed. Taron was very up for going the whole hog. He was willing to shave his head and remove part of his hair so that we could then put balding wigs and stuff like that on him. With Taron, it's really uncanny how much he actually looks like Elton once we did that. When Elton himself saw one of the first pictures that was released he thought it was a picture of himself. So that's a real compliment!"

Below Left Egerton takes a break between takes; pictured in his on-set trailer.

Below Right A key restaurant scene between Elton and his parents calls for an emotional performance.

Bottom Elton backstage at the Troubadour.

Opposite Egerton in one of Elton's more subtle onstage costumes.

Overleaf Taron as Elton: photography by David LaChapelle.

"I'VE SHAVED MY HAIRLINE BACK, THINNED MY HAIR … BUT THE COSTUMES HAVE NEVER MADE ME FEEL LIKE I'VE HAD TO LEAVE MY DIGNITY AT THE DOOR." TARON EGERTON

★ CHAPTER 3: **SHOOTING STARS**

SHOOTING STARS

Casting the main players of *Rocketman* began in April 2018 and, very quickly, the roll call of characters began to be filled with some of the hottest young actors working today, not to mention a few familiar faces, from both the US and UK.

JAMIE BELL AS BERNIE TAUPIN

Bell and Elton's working relationship began back at the dawn of the millennium, when Jamie was 13, with Stephen Daldry's *Billy Elliot*, also written by *Rocketman* scribe Lee Hall.
   For Fletcher, Bell had the right "grounded' qualities to bounce off Egerton's flamboyant Elton. "Jamie was right for me for that because there's an earthiness that I was really interested in counterpointing. It allowed Taron to fly into these extraordinary places, but that he always had this grounded anchor that just keeps hold of the rope, and stops him flying out into the atmosphere and getting completely lost."

Above and **Opposite** "Bernie was very grounded, he knew who he was. Whereas Elton was someone forever trying to grab onto some identity." Jamie Bell.

"I THOUGHT IF AN ELTON JOHN STORY WAS GOING TO BE TOLD, THIS IS EXACTLY HOW IT SHOULD BE TOLD. IT'S THE RIGHT TONE, IT'S COLOURFUL, IT'S VIBRANT, IT'S PSYCHEDELIC, IT'S DARK. I WAS JUST OVER THE MOON THAT DEXTER WANTED TO BRING ME ALONG FOR IT AS WELL."

JAMIE BELL

Above Elton John and Bernie Taupin's songwriting relationship has lasted for 50 years.

Opposite "I love you, man…but not in that way." Egerton and Bell re-enact a moving scene from the movie.

RICHARD MADDEN AS JOHN REID

Richard Madden portrays John Reid, Elton's first boyfriend of five years, and also his manager for 28 years. Lines were blurred, and the relationship soon became toxic. Sophisticated and cunning, Madden gives a realness to Reid's enigma. "Their relationship gives Elton a lot of his confidence in being able to be out and be himself and be in a relationship with a man. As the film goes on, John becomes the villain."

"I'D LIKE RICHARD MADDEN TO PLAY ME IN A MOVIE, HE LOOKS FUCKING GREAT."

DEXTER FLETCHER

Above and **Opposite** Richard Madden as John Reid, the handsome, dashing businessman.

BRYCE DALLAS HOWARD
AS SHEILA FAREBROTHER

The last of the cast to join the movie, Bryce Dallas Howard wanted in the very second she finished reading the script. "I was on camera six days later," she revealed. "When we first meet my character, it is with the introduction of the song *The Bitch Is Back*. So, that kind of explains her vibe!" quips Howard. "Sheila was a woman who had a toxic relationship with Elton John's biological father. Elton was raised in this environment with two people who hated each other, and who were willing to wedge him in between the other person."

> "I UNDERSTOOD IMMEDIATELY THAT WHAT
> I NEEDED WAS A REALLY STRONG FEMALE
> CHARACTER THAT DIDN'T NEED A LOT OF
> SETTING UP AND BRYCE BROUGHT ALL OF
> THAT TO BEAR WITHIN JUST HER FIRST LINE."
>
> DEXTER FLETCHER

Opposite and **Above** Bryce Dallas Howard brings a bit of sunny Hollywood starpower to Pinner's grey suburbs.

STEPHEN GRAHAM AS DICK JAMES

Notorious 1960s music publisher Dick James is the person who brought Elton and Bernie together and gave the pair their first big break. "James already had a successful run with the Beatles," explains Graham, "and he nurtured Elton in the beginning, taking him under his wing. He had a soft spot for Elton; they all used to call him Uncle Dick."

Opposite and **Above** "He could be cut-throat when he wanted to be, but he was a nice fellow by all accounts," said Graham of his character, Dick James.

STEVEN MACKINTOSH AS STANLEY DWIGHT

The main emotional motivation of the film is Elton's relationship with Stanley Dwight, his biological father. Elton lies that his father "hugged him all the time", when in reality Stanley was cold and unloving towards Elton, and unable to show his son any emotion… except resentment.

Opposite and **Above** Military man Stanley Dwight was cynical of young Reggie's musical talents.

GEMMA JONES AS IVY SEWELL

In Gemma Jones, *Rocketman* finds its beating heart. "They were very close, Elton and Ivy,"
explains Jones. "She was a great supporter and very loyal and loving. It was Ivy who found
him a piano teacher, and really encouraged his musical education. Whereas Sheila was
very selfish and not particularly interested and didn't like the noise in the house."

TOM BENNETT AS FRED FAREBROTHER

Fred, or Derf, as Elton would affectionately call his stepfather, was a rock 'n' roller who
came into Reggie's life at the age of eight. "He is actually quite a nice, early supportive figure in
Reggie's life, who turned him onto rock 'n' roll a bit, gave him a bit of a push," reveals Bennett.

MATTHEW ILLESLEY AS YOUNG REGGIE

Six-year-old Reggie, portrayed by young actor Matthew Illesley, is "very mischievous"
says the actor. Illesley will long remember appearing in his first film for "meeting all
the famous people…and the joy of being in it."

KIT CONNOR AS OLDER REGGIE

There are three ages of Elton in *Rocketman*. Kit Connor plays the middle one, when Reggie
is 12 years old, beginning to fall in love with rock 'n' roll piano, vinyl records and Elvis Presley.
"He's very used to being in the shadows because of his mother's big personality, and his father
is very strict," says Connor of his character.

DEXTER FLETCHER

With Fletcher on board for *Rocketman*, it was assured that the film would have heart and energy, as that is how the cast and crew describe their "lovely" director. "Dexter was just all over this story," recalls Bell. "He knew exactly what it was and how extraordinary it had to be, because he understands Elton very well. And he's unafraid. That's the best thing about Dexter – he is unafraid of committing things to film that might be controversial or outrageous."

Below Dexter Fletcher sees the funny side on set.
Opposite Above Dexter and Taron talk over a piano, preparing for the movie's final scene.
Opposite Below Director Dexter Fletcher, Producer Adam Bohling and Cinematographer George Richmond.

"GOING TO SEE THIS MOVIE IS LIKE GOING TO AN ELTON JOHN CONCERT, BECAUSE IT'S NOT JUST ONE SONG AFTER THE NEXT, A STORY IS TOLD. ELTON'S A REMARKABLE, BRILLIANT AND A VERY EMOTIONAL STORYTELLER." BRYCE DALLAS HOWARD

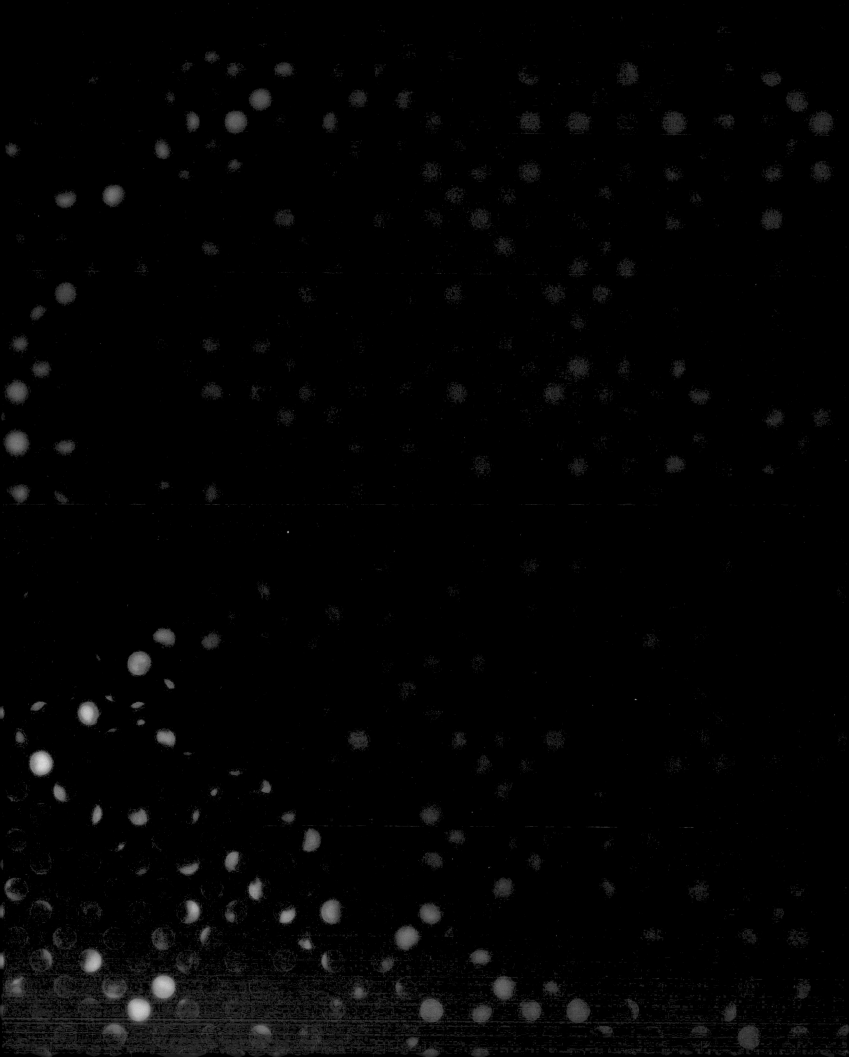

★ CHAPTER 4: **THIS IS MY SONG**

★

THIS IS MY SONG

Working in collaboration with acclaimed music producer Giles Martin, Fletcher and his crew have brought to life an incredible selection of Elton's most inspiring tracks in a way never before heard. Let's shine a spotlight on the songs and their scenes…

THE BITCH IS BACK

The opening song of *Rocketman* is a fierce reimagining of Elton's classic 1972 rocker. Transported from Parklands Hospital in the present to Pinner Close, in 1950s London, Elton and young Reggie join in with a group dance on the streets outside Sheila and Ivy's suburban home with the milkman, the postman and lollipop lady, as well as Elton's rehab group. The scene brings together the characters of Elton's past, present and future – a trick that shows the viewer that they're in for a wild ride. "I chose *The Bitch Is Back*" revealed Fletcher, "because it very clearly sets out our stall that this film is going to be something you don't expect."

"WE WERE LUCKY ENOUGH TO BE GRANTED PERMISSION TO REINVENT THESE SONGS IN THE WAY THAT WE NEEDED TO TELL THE STORY." DEXTER FLETCHER

Above The opening number sets out the film's stall from the very beginning, both visually and sonically.

Opposite Dexter and Taron on set, deep in discussion on how best to stage *The Bitch Is Back*.

I WANT LOVE

In Sheila's house, young Reggie, Sheila and Ivy all declare their desire for love as Stanley stares out the window. The characters sing a reimagined *I Want Love*. "I want love, but it's impossible. A man like him, so irresponsible. A man like him is dead in places," Reggie sings about his unloving father. "When you hear a song like *I Want Love*, you hear a really lovely pop standard," says Fletcher, "but when you apply it to a particular dramatic moment it becomes an incredible storytelling device. The song was written after our film ends, but I can place it in 1957, when I need to tell my story."

Below Reggie, Sheila and Ivy discuss the aspiring pianist's place at the Royal Academy of Music.
Bottom Reggie learns his scales.

SATURDAY NIGHT'S ALRIGHT (FOR FIGHTING)

The provenance of Elton's passion for performance begins at the Northwood pub, in Pinner, where pre-teenage Reggie would play piano. In this montage scene for *Saturday Night's Alright (For Fighting)*, Reggie's awesome honky-tonk kick-starts a pub fight.

Above Reggie leaves the Northwood to take the fight to the streets at the start of one of the film's stand-out musical numbers.

53★

YOUR SONG

The moment Elton pens the music to *Your Song* at the piano in Sheila's house is an integral moment in the film: it shows the love Bernie has for Elton and their unique working relationship. Tom Bennet, (Fred Farebrother in the movie) remembers the scene: "Bernie just passes Elton the lyrics, Elton sits down, they're all having breakfast. Bernie goes upstairs to shave. Elton just starts playing the notes, finding it. And before you know it, it's *Your Song*. And everyone stands there and watches *Your Song* being created. It's a beautiful scene."

Below Left Moneyless Elton composes the music to *Your Song*, wearing a dressing gown. It would be the last time he would wear something so ordinary at a piano.
Below Right Bernie Taupin's handwritten lyrics to *Your Song*.
Bottom Egerton learnt to play the piano for the role.
Opposite Bernie and Elton reluctantly move back to Pinner.

CROCODILE ROCK

In the movie, Elton's breakout US performance of *Crocodile Rock* was at L.A.'s iconic venue the Troubadour, owned and operated by Dick James' friend, Doug Weston. As the script tells us, Elton gives "a performance of a lifetime… the whole energy and power of the music and performance is lifting everyone and everything up in the air." And that is, literally, what happens.

Above Elton (Egerton) surveys L.A.'s "really cool folk club."

Below Just 300 people were in attendance on August 25, 1970 – the night everything changed for Elton. In reality he didn't play *Crocodile Rock*.

Opposite Backstage set design and pre-show excitement with Elton and Bernie. "It's time to do something bold!" Dick James told the duo.

Above Egerton (pre-flight) at the piano singing *Crocodile Rock*.

Opposite The movie version of the poster. advertising Elton's six-night run at the Troubadour.

Overleaf Egerton in flight.

TINY DANCER

Following Elton's classic *Crocodile Rock* performance at the Troubadour, Bernie and Elton are invited to Mama Cass's (of the Mama and the Papas) house in the hills above L.A. It is here that Elton starts to feel lost and alone among all the madness. He breaks into a reimagining of *Tiny Dancer*. "We use the song as a way of showing an introspective interlude in Elton's evening at Mama Cass's party; he's reflecting and processing the fact that Bernie isn't just his and that being grown up means that things don't always go your way."

Below Egerton ready for the opening line of *Tiny Dancer*.
Bottom The moment Elton and John Reid meet for the first time. There's fireworks.
Opposite "How cool is this?" Elton surveys the L.A. party scene and ponders his place among the cool people.
Overleaf Reconstructing Elton and Kiki Dee recording the all-time classic *Don't Go Breaking My Heart*.

HONKY CAT

Elton and John Reid's "showstopping number" begins when Reid, ironically, pushes Elton into a closet. This three-minute song highlights the early years of Elton and Reid's relationship, where Reid "introduced Elton to the finer things in life." Naturally, it's all played out as a big dance number, as the two men are surrounded by expensive possessions, houses, food and drink.

Below Elton and Reid ready for dessert.

"WE DON'T JUST GO GOSPEL BY THE SONGS, WE REWORKED AND REIMAGINED AND PLAYED AROUND WITH THEM. WE MADE THEM FIT THE DIALOGUE SO THAT WE DON'T DO THE CLUNKY OUT OF DIALOGUE INTO MUSICAL NUMBERS THING." DEXTER FLETCHER

PINBALL WIZARD

In this highly visually exciting scene, Elton enters a montage sequence of tours and making huge amounts of money. Elton is blindly bounced and buffered from one concert to another.

Above Elton alone, during a scene with John Reid which inspired the *Pinball Wizard* sequence in the film.

ROCKET MAN

Elton hits the bottom, but continues to sink even lower when he crashes, after taking an overdose, head first into the swimming pool at his L.A. home, surrounded by Ivy, Sheila and Fred and other friends. Once at the bottom of the pool, the singer dives into the opening line of *Rocket Man*. He is rushed to hospital.

Below Scene 132 sees Elton sink to the bottom of his pool. "And for my next trick, I'm going to drown myself," he tells the party.
Opposite Ivy, Sheila and Fred (and the Andersons from next door) visit Elton in L.A.

"DEXTER PLAYED ME TARON SINGING *ROCKET MAN* AND THAT'S WHAT MADE ME REALLY EXCITED ABOUT THIS MOVIE. I THOUGHT, 'OK, IF TARON'S GOING TO DO THIS, AND DEXTER'S GOING TO DO THAT, THEN WE COULD HAVE SOMETHING REALLY EXCITING ON OUR HANDS.'"

RICHARD MADDEN

Above Elton, pulled from the pool after sinking deeper than the bottom.

Below "Elton really did actually jump in the pool the day before the Dodger Stadium gig," said Egerton.

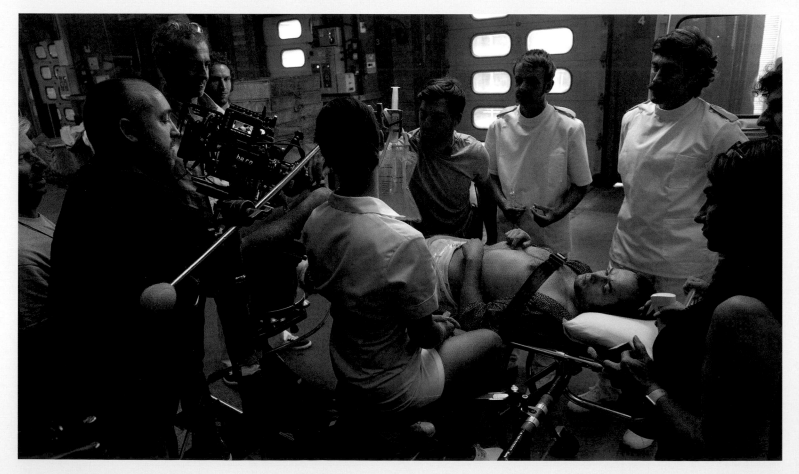

BENNIE AND THE JETS

The opening music to Elton's iconic 1973 track commences in the clouds aboard the *Starship*, before plunging into the underground depths of the Wonderland, a gay club in 1980s New York. Elton meets the character Bennie, as portrayed by Jake Shears of the Scissor Sisters.

"*Bennie and the Jets* was always the jewel in the crown of the film and intended to be a real showstopper," says Egerton. "If *Honky Cat* is the seed of excess, *Bennie and the Jets* is the finished oak of things. We arrive at a point where Elton's life no longer feels glamorous."

Below Left "We should take a break." Elton and Bernie come to the end of the Yellow Brick Road.

Below Right "Glasses are very important to Elton," said costume designer Julian Day. "There were a few that I really wanted to remake and re-envisage."

Bottom "Dexter took a little convincing with the hot pants," remembers Egerton.

DON'T LET THE SUN GO DOWN ON ME

Performed initially a cappella at a piano by Elton and then-girlfriend Renate at a London recording studio, it concludes with a gospel choir as the pair get married, to the obvious confusion of Taupin, Reid and Elton's family. "Under this banner of the film being magical fantasy, I don't need to have big scenes of dialogue to tell a story, I can just do it in a dramatic moment where Renate and Elton sing *Don't Let the Sun Go Down On Me* as a duet at a piano; the audience will understand the significance," explains Fletcher.

Below Producers David Furnish and Adam Bohling visited the set the day Elton (Egerton) married Renate (Celinde Schoenmaker).

Opposite A confusing day for all concerned. "I dragged her into all that madness," Elton says in the film, of his three-year marriage.

> "AUDIENCES WANT FILMS THAT ARE FULL OF SPECTACLE AND ESCAPISM. AND IF WE CAN DO THAT WITH A MUSICAL, AND TELL ELTON'S STORY, THEN WE GET TWO FILMS FOR THE PRICE OF ONE." DEXTER FLETCHER

SORRY SEEMS TO BE THE HARDEST WORD

As Elton reaches his lowest ebb, full of self-loathing and plagued by addictions, the film cues, rather aptly, *Sorry Seems to be the Hardest Word* on the jukebox. "Nobody hates you…" Bernie tells Elton at one of London's fanciest restaurants. "…Nobody except you."

Below Left Elton, dressed in his *The Wizard of Oz*-inspired outfit, prepares for a verbal scrap with Bernie.

Below Elton storms out on to the streets of Piccadilly as *Goodbye Yellow Brick Road* kicks in.

Bottom Fletcher runs through this important scene with his leading men.

GOODBYE YELLOW BRICK ROAD

The scene for *Goodbye Yellow Brick Road* is set at a glitzy London restaurant, following on from a previous restaurant scene, where Elton and Bernie get into a serious disagreement. Bernie sings to his friend, the Rocketman: "When are you going to come down / When are you going to land?" but Elton isn't listening. "This is the song where Elton and I are coming apart," recalls Bell. "I sing *Goodbye Yellow Brick Road*, as if Elton will find a replacement, like there's plenty of lyricists like me to be found."

Above The beginning of the end (of the film) starts as Elton confronts who he has become. "I'm sick of running away from who I am," the singer shouts at Sheila. "I don't live life in black and white."

I'M STILL STANDING

The film's finale kicks in with the chords of Elton's 1983 rocker, *I'm Still Standing*. Elton, dressed in white suit and boater, from the song's signature music video, is at the centre of his rehab group in Parklands Hospital. He is transformed, clean, healthy and drug free. This is the happy ending viewers have been waiting for.

"For *I'm Still Standing* we take on a very iconic Elton look," explains Egerton. "Elton puts his boater on in his bedroom, and magically appears in the therapy room and starts singing to no one in particular. But there's something kind of quite fun and kooky and weird about it, and it turns into a big showstopping number to finish the film."

Above Egerton straightens his tie as he prepares for the final showstopping number.
Below Costume professionals ensure Egerton looks perfect.

Right Elton, standing tall.
Overleaf Egerton prepares for the movie's climactic moment.

REIMAGINING ELTON ☆

GILES MARTIN

At the end of summer 2018, Grammy award-winning producer and composer Giles Martin was brought on board to produce the reimagining of *Rocketman*'s songs, including writing the arrangements. When it came to adapting the songs for the film, "all bets were off," said Fletcher. "The songs are here to service us. We're not there to create a platform for Elton to perform songs – these songs are there at our disposal like the set design is, like the costume design is, like the lighting design – and having someone like Giles, who understands how that vision works, and bringing all his power to bear as well, elevates it all."

Opposite Above The extroverted introvert meets Reggie. "When are you going to hug me?" his younger self asks.

Opposite Below The cameras close in on Egerton's revealing, heartfelt performance. A vital scene.

Below Taron Egerton, working in the studio with Music Producer Giles Martin.

★ CHAPTER 5: **THE WORLD'S A STAGE**

★

THE WORLD'S A STAGE

For an artist who famously sang *I'm Still Standing*, Elton John did a fabulous job of never actually standing still. Seemingly endless world tours meant that Elton's life was a revolving reel of international jet-setting. For *Rocketman*, the producers choose just a handful of locations that represent defining moments in the singer's life and music.

SHEILA'S HOUSE

"We start off with Elton's childhood home in Pinner which is set in the 1950s," explains *Rocketman*'s production designer Marcus Rowland. It is in this house that young Reggie understands that his family life is far from perfect, so he dreams of performing Tchaikovsky with an orchestra at the end of his bed. "We wanted to make it period accurate, so everything's slightly muted and sombre. The fifties, that period in time, was a tiny bit more austere anyway and there wasn't that volume of colour that was available. So it's got a very brown tone."

Left Sheila (Bryce Dallas Howard) and son, young Reggie, played by newcomer Matthew Illesley.
Below "Dexter's funny. He makes jokes, which makes it a joy to work with him," Illesley says of his director.
Bottom Dream scene: Reggie and his bedroom orchestra.

"You're late! I've had to throw your dinner in the bin. Get inside!"

"Life gives you very few chances, Reggie. This is one of yours."

ROYAL ACADEMY OF MUSIC

People often forget that Elton is a classically trained pianist, having studied for a time when he was a boy at London's Royal Academy of Music. He was encouraged to pursue his natural talent by his piano teacher, Helen Piena, and grandmother Ivy. "I was so keen to try and get the actual Royal Academy of Music as a location and shoot it for what it was," said Fletcher. "I made contact with them and told them what the project was. They were super excited and they said we could shoot an interior and exterior."

Top Left and **Top Right** "You've got a great future here," Royal Academy of Music teacher Helen Piena schools Reggie.

Above Left Ivy encourages Reggie to get over his shy silliness. "Play at being confident," she says. "You're good at that, aren't you?"

Above Right Elton and Helen Piena discuss rock 'n' roll and dirty pubs, in a scene that didn't make the movie's final edit.

CUL-DE-SAC: PINNER CLOSE

Described as an "archetypal suburban scene" in the script, the big dance number of *The Bitch Is Back* most definitely wakes up the sleepy neighbours. "*The Bitch Is Back* starts with Elton in rehab, and him beginning to tell the story of his childhood," says Adam Murray, the film's choreographer. "We approached this scene from the view that Elton was going to tell everybody this unrealistic ideal of what his childhood upbringing was. So we wanted him to step out of those rehab doors, and him to be in the most beautiful, happy, cheery, Pleasantville-type land in 1950s Pinner. Young Reggie goes on to have this relationship with all of his neighbours, and the people in his community, that obviously wasn't real. The song ends with his mum, Sheila, coming out and shouting at Reggie which is a really funny way to end the number."

"He's not the bitch, I am."

Above Six-year-old Reggie transports the audience back to 1950s Pinner.

Below Egerton brings colour to the "humdrum drabness of 1950s London," said Fletcher.

Above The devil and young Reggie meet outside the house Elton grew up in.

Opposite Showdown in suburbia.

Left The devil cools off with an ice cream.

Middle The streets of suburbia are alive with the sound of *The Bitch Is Back*.

Bottom Fletcher discussing a piano moment with Young Reggie.

Above Shot on location in Pinner, a stone's throw from the road Elton grew up in.

Below Left Elton's past catches up with his present. Will the future save the day?

Below Right Shooting on a real residential street in Pinner presented some "logistical challenges".

Opposite "I mean, there's no escaping that costume, is there?" says Marcus Rowland.

DENMARK STREET

As Elton's voice began to be heard, Tin Pan Alley, or Denmark Street, in London's Soho, was becoming the epicentre of the city's growing rock 'n' roll scene. It was close by, on New Oxford Street, that Elton famously signed with Dick James, giving Elton his first foray into music.

"THERE'S NOT ONE SET IN THE FILM THAT LOOKS LIKE A SET. AND FOR ME THAT'S LIKE A MASSIVE ACHIEVEMENT. I DEFY ANYONE TO SAY 'OH, THAT'S DEFINITELY A SET.'"

DEXTER FLETCHER

ALL SAINTS ROAD

"Ah, my wonderful new lodgers. They're struggling rock stars," says Arabella, welcoming Bernie and Elton into her flat, a sort of bohemian squat, occupied by tenants Clint, a rasta, and Arthur, a very small man. The song-writing duo move to Arabella's as they require a house in central London to live "rent free" that isn't with Elton's mum. It's not long before Elton realizes Arabella fancies him, "for some reason", and he is forced to "bunk" with her. It's not long either, before they're thrown out.

Above Fletcher runs through the scene at Arabella's All Saints Road flat. Many of these location scenes were deleted from the film.

Left Arabella, Elton's first love interest in the film.

Opposite Above Arabella, Clint and Arthur welcome their two new lodgers.

Opposite Below "Your voice is what I hear when I write," Bernie tells Elton. "You're an artist."

THE LANCASTER GRILL

"As it's known in Pimlico today, the Regency, is a very busy café. But it was a very good location to shoot Bernie and Elton's first proper scene together," explains Fletcher. The café in question is dressed as a greasy spoon, though it's a lot nicer in real life.

This key scene sees the duo begin their fifty-year career with Elton poring over a pile of Bernie's handwritten lyrics. As Egerton reveals: "They meet in the Lancaster Grill and talk about cowboys. And it's lovely, these two young Milky Bar kids, meeting for the first time." It's at this moment that Elton realizes he has met his soul brother.

The scene is mirrored towards the climax of the movie, when Bernie and Elton meet for the final time, in a luxury restaurant, and fail to see eye to eye. "At that point, they're two ageing gunslingers, and there is an element of this which is a western. There is a sense that they're cowboys facing off over a table," says Egerton.

Below Elton and Bernie discuss music and lyrics at the Lancaster Grill.

STANLEY'S HOUSE

Proving that you can never go home, Elton's trip to meet Stanley at his new family home does not bring the closure Elton had hoped. "There's a scene, early in the film, where Reggie approaches Stanley, and his father's listening to a record and young Reggie pulls out a record and says, 'What's this one, dad?' And his father's incredibly icy and says, 'put that back. Don't ever touch my records again'," explains Steven Mackintosh, the actor who portrays Stanley. "But, later on, when Elton goes to see his father and pulls up in a gold Rolls-Royce, wearing massive platform boots and a glittery top and massive glasses, and meets Stanley ensconced with a new family, Stanley asks his young sons to go and fetch his Elton record and asks if he'll sign it. For Elton, it's all a bit like 'What is going on? This is very, very strange and quite painful.'"

"The boys loved meeting a real life pop star."

Right Egerton as Elton meeting his father Stanley and his two new sons.

WOODSIDE

Elton John and David Furnish's house, Woodside, features in the film in key scenes where Elton and Renate get married (and quickly separate), as well as being the location of many of Elton's intoxicated moments, including a memorable scene where Elton slides face first down the large staircase. "We actually recced Elton's house, Woodside, to see what the interior was like," reveals Fletcher. "We had a look around, trying to understand the feel of it. We ultimately shot at Brocket Hall, Hertfordshire, a good match for the interior and exterior."

Below Elton and Reid fight at Woodside, the singer's home, in a deleted scene.   **Right** A close approximation of Elton's Woodside – Brocket Hall, Hertfordshire.

THE STARSHIP

Designed to look as little like a plane as possible, the *Starship* was a United Airlines Boeing 720 passenger jet that was leased by rock stars such as Led Zeppelin, Deep Purple and the Rolling Stones, among others, in the mid 1970s.

With its fully-stocked bar, 30-foot long couch, revolving armchairs and electric organ, the *Starship* was the ultimate icon of rock star extravagance and success.

Below If these walls could talk: Elton aboard the legendary *Starship*.

CHAPTER 6: **THE SHY BOY FROM PINNER**

THE SHY BOY FROM PINNER

Rocketman takes the cast and crew, and the viewer, all over the world and spans four different decades. However, Elton's story begins, rather unsurprisingly, at his mother's home on a quiet road in Pinner, in 1950s London, where residents just go round and round in their daily lives. Naturally, it doesn't take young Reggie long to break free of the cycle.

A NIGHT DOWN THE PUB

Known as the 'SNAFF' scene among the cast and crew, the filming of the Northwood pub fight, and resulting funfair scene which accompanies the belter *Saturday Night's Alright (For Fighting)*, soon became a highlight of the shoot. "It's a smoky sort of dirty, dingy, classic sort of London pub," explains Marcus Rowland, production designer, "where Elton's very much playing the piano in the background. It's Elton's first taste of the glamorous side of the music industry!"

> "Tonight: All meat raffle plus Reginald Dwight on the piano!"

ALL THE FUN OF THE FAIR

"The funfair was my idea," remembers Fletcher. "Getting Elton out in the alleyway, away from the pub and getting him to a funfair was all about creating something that felt current. So, when you have run Elton down an alleyway into a funfair and transform him into the 17-year-old version of himself you get to see the genesis of his musical influences together all in one place."

Opposite "Play that one I like," Ivy tells Elton as he performs *Saturday Night's Alright (For Fighting)* at the Northwood pub.

Above Elton meets, and embraces, all walks of London life at the funfair.

Right Taron Egerton prepares for his first big song and dance number.

Opposite Above The funfair scene is a seamless transition between 14-year-old Reggie (Kit Connor) into Egerton, who plays 17-year-old Reggie.

Oppposite Below, **Below** and **Overleaf** "We wanted this scene to be a feast for the eyes," reveals Fletcher. "An overpowering sense of youth culture."

"FOR *SATURDAY NIGHT'S ALRIGHT (FOR FIGHTING)* WE GO THROUGH THE JOURNEY IN THE FUNFAIR, AND WE COME ACROSS THE TEDS, THE MODS, BHANGRA, SKA, AND ALL OF THOSE MUSICAL INFLUENCES THAT WERE IMPORTANT IN THE STORYTELLING AT THAT PART OF ELTON'S LIFE, WHERE HE'S BEEN IMMERSED IN 1950S LONDON."

DEXTER FLETCHER

"Gonna set this dance alight."

"I'm a juvenile product of the working class."

BLUESOLOGY TOUR

Following the formation of Bluesology, Elton and the group are offered a six-month tour of northern working men's clubs with the Bell Blues Quintet. For the film, this story of Elton's earliest touring is told in montage sequence, accompanied by the song *Breaking Down the Walls of Heartache*. "We're shooting in a real working men's club. Very faithful to the kind of places that Elton would have been playing at this time in his life. It's got that kind of earthy charm, shall we say," remembers Fletcher.

Below Left A poster advertising the American Soul Tour, supported by Bluesology.

Below Right "The sound of the future. Your future." Elton on a six-month UK tour with US soul group The Bell Blues Quintet.

Bottom "Tough negotiators" Bluesology talk terms with music promoter Dave Godin.

Opposite Elton John learning his craft.

★ CHAPTER 7: **FROM LONDON TO L.A.**

LONDON TO L.A.

In act two of *Rocketman*, Elton and Bernie swap the roads of Pinner for the London streets paved with gold. But as the film swan dives into the 1970s, Elton soon realizes he's the star of his own show and packs his bags pre-flight for L.A. But, as Dick James tells him bluntly, "America's a gamble. If you fuck it up, I'll kill you."

THE TROUBADOUR

"The Troubadour is where Elton has this defining moment for him where the energy lifts everybody off the ground, it becomes elevated and that's really sort of like the jumping off point for all the fantastical elements of the film," reveals Fletcher. "Once I knew that the storytelling allowed me to totally indulge all my crazy ideas then I knew I had a really great platform to just be really crazy. And because of the nature of who Elton is, and who we understand him to be, it's natural that you would want to do something fantastical."

Preceding this vital scene, Elton enjoys his first foray into flamboyant fashion – acquiring a pair of sparkling wedge platform boots. Not exactly what Dick James had in mind when he told Elton, "Get yourself some new clothes, something flashy, put on a great fucking show, and don't kill yourself with drugs."

Below Elton belts out *Crocodile Rock*.
Opposite Above Elton ready to take off at the Troubadour show, August 25, 1970.
Opposite Below John Reid (Madden) keeps his eyes on the prize.
Overleaf Egerton suspended in mid-air during the scene's most uplifting moment.

"And now, ladies and gentlemen, a rising star of rock 'n' roll all the way from London, England. Please welcome Elton John!"

DODGER STADIUM

The Dodger Stadium story has now become an ingrained part of rock 'n' roll legend. Two nights before Elton performs the first of his now iconic, if infamous, sold-out US stadium shows at Dodger Stadium, L.A., the singer overdoses and is rushed to hospital. The day of the first gig, Elton is back and performs to 55,000 fans who are none the wiser. He played it again the next night too.

"It's a particularly dark point in Elton's history, this suicide bid," recalls Egerton. "He is at a point in his life where he is indulging too much, and it all kind of comes to a head for him here."

Above Fletcher and Egerton keep the conversation serious.

Left The Dodger Stadium audience will arrive in post-production.

Opposite Egerton before the big Dodger Stadium scene.

Above and **Below** Moments before "shooting up into the air like a rocket," Elton knocks it out of the park.

MAMA CASS'S PARTY, LAUREL CANYON, L.A.

Immediately following the overwhelming success of Elton's showcase concert at the Troubadour, Bernie and Elton are invited to party at Mama Cass's house (actually shot in Amersham, UK, not L.A.) "Bernie meets a young woman, and has this very exciting first sexual experience with her," recounts Egerton. "Elton's left not quite knowing where his place is, and what things hold for him, so he experiences a moment of loneliness and introspection, told through the song *Tiny Dancer*."

Rather serendipitously after the song concludes, Elton meets the dashing John Reid and the pair share a moment together, and a bed. Before they kiss, Reid predicts the future by telling Elton, "You don't realize what happened at the Troubadour tonight, do you? There are moments in a rock star's life that define who he is and how people perceive him as he ascends into the heavens. You lit the blue touch paper and now we can all see you throwing light and colour and magic into the night sky. Where there was darkness, there is now you, Elton John. You can be anyone you want. And it's going to be a wild ride."

> "Hey Elton. How cool is this?"
> "Yeah, great. Apparently Dylan is here somewhere."

Opposite Fletcher sets an authentic looking Laurel Canyon, L.A., scene…shot in the UK.

Above and Below Fletcher and his blue jean baby.
Overleaf Elton is the odd one out.

ELTON'S L.A. MANSION: THE ROCKETMAN ENTERS

It's at his magnificent L.A. mansion that Elton takes a dive into the deep end and reaches his lowest point. Shot not in L.A. but at Brookmans Park, near Potters Bar, London. "The first place we look at, anywhere, when they say L.A. is Potters Bar," quips Fletcher. "The biggest challenge of shooting in the UK, and not L.A., is the weather and getting the palm trees and swimming pool right," says Fletcher. The swimming pool had to be just right, as it is the location of the film's most heart-breaking moment – when *Rocket Man* kicks in.

Opposite "Where am I?" Elton plunges into a dark place.
Below The drugs don't work.
Bottom Elton points out his lack of success on the charts to Reid.

133★

CHAPTER 8: **FOR MY NEXT TRICK**

FOR MY NEXT TRICK

At the beginning of act three, Elton finds himself at the top of the downward spiral that would carry him through the late 1970s into the early 1980s...and ultimately into the rehab that saved his life.

TRIPPING THE CASH FANTASTIC

For Elton John and John Reid's big dance number, Dexter Fletcher envisioned the pair dancing through a variety of scenes, in the film's biggest and most spectacular set piece, one that defines Elton and Reid's relationship and allows the song *Honky Cat* to be heard as never before.

The scene becomes a flamboyant song and dance routine, although the top hat section of the number did not make it into the final edit of the movie. Fletcher wanted to take the grace of *Singing in the Rain* and "flip it on its head and make it all about opulence and self-indulgence, and all about the spending of money." He continues: "Elton John was responsible for five per cent of all records sold at one point. That's an incredible amount of money, so the song needed to celebrate and look at that, because that was his reality at that point. But it's also about his detachment from reality."

Below Filming a song and dance number from a subsequently deleted scene.
Opposite Elton is fitted for a suit by dancing tailors.

> "You're a millionaire rock star who lives at home with his mum. This is grown up time now. Things are serious. Be brave. Think big. What do you really want?"

UNDERGROUND WONDERLAND

At the height of his drug addiction, Elton John was feeling his lowest. Everything had got out of hand and the singer's life had become a revolving door of lovers, lines and limos. The hardcore partying finally descends underground to the Wonderland club in New York City, where Elton is seen indulging in his every desire. Complete with a big staircase which Elton descends into the wild throng of lovers and revellers. "It's very… very glitzy, basically, and very over the top. Very 80s," explains Marcus Rowland. "Wonderland is the high point or the low point depending on your viewpoint," begins Fletcher. "It's the point in this story where Elton loses himself."

Below Elton and entourage arrive at Wonderland.
Opposite Above The club welcomes its king.
Opposite Below Elton meets "excessive characters" such as Bennie as he walks through the club.
Overleaf "The *Bennie and the Jets* scene is about drugs and sex … and actually not a lot about rock and roll," revealed Egerton during filming.

"I CAN'T DO A WARTS-AND-ALL IF I DON'T SHOW THE WARTS." DEXTER FLETCHER

PARKLANDS HOSPITAL

Following Elton's realization that his life is in a destructive spiral, he heads to Parklands to clear his head with rehab. The truth is, he's been there the whole film. It's only now, he's found himself again, that he chooses to leave. The action returns to Parklands frequently throughout the course of the film, allowing Elton to reveal, or lie about, how he felt about certain elements of his own story with the viewer, and his rehab group.

It was shot at Bakerbrie Mansion in Hertfordshire, which doubles as the US drug rehabilitation facility. "When we found this location, it felt perfect," says Fletcher. "You can see the nurses outside, wheeling wheelchairs, old men in wheelchairs and all that kind of stuff."

> "IT'S IN THE THERAPY GROUP THERE THAT ELTON RECOUNTS THE STORY OF HIS LIFE AND EXORCIZES HIS DEMONS AND COMES TO TERMS WITH HIMSELF AND ULTIMATELY STARTS HIS ROAD TO RECOVERY. IN HIS MIND, HE'S VISITED BY ALL OF THE PRIME MOVERS IN HIS LIFE, HIS FAMILY AND HIS FRIENDS, THE PEOPLE WHO HAVE BEEN INSTRUMENTAL ON HIS JOURNEY TO BECOMING ELTON JOHN."
>
> TARON EGERTON

Right Elton emerges from rehab, triumphant and ready to sing.

★ CHAPTER 9

THE BIGGEST PLATFORM BOOTS KNOWN TO MAN

THE BIGGEST PLATFORM BOOTS
KNOWN TO MAN

Taron Egerton delights in his incredible portrayal of Elton John. But it is the costumes he wears, designed by Julian Day, that truly define the character as fierce, fascinating and forever original.

THE DEVIL

"This is the costume that appears first and last in the film," says Julian Day. "It was the costume that I first designed, and it was the one that was in my head. I had a dream about it."

It's in the 'devil costume' that Elton decides very suddenly that his excesses have become untenable and he decides to go to rehab. "His struggle between light and dark is manifested in the costume," says Egerton.

Below "It has elements of the devil, and it has elements of the angelic," says Egerton of his devil costume.
Opposite The devil takes a break.

"COSTUME IS A LOT LIKE ARMOUR FOR ELTON. AS HE RECOUNTS HIS EXPERIENCES, HE BEGINS THE HEALING PROCESS; AS HE GROWS MORE COMFORTABLE, HE BEGINS TO TAKE THINGS OFF. BY THE END OF THE FILM, IT'S HIM IN JUST A VERY FLUFFY, WARM DRESSING GOWN, WITH NOTHING BUT HIS GLASSES ON. AND IT'S SYMBOLIC OF HIS GROWTH THROUGHOUT THE STORY."

TARON EGERTON

FLOWER POWER

In the sixties, Elton took his Bluesology band on a six-month tour across the UK.
It was here that he met lots of "jazzily dressed" Americans who inspired Elton's clothing
choices throughout this period. The drab colours wouldn't last.

"*ROCKETMAN* IS AN ABSOLUTE DREAM JOB FOR A COSTUME DESIGNER.
I THINK IT'S A DREAM JOB FOR ANYBODY THAT'S WORKING ON IT."

JULIAN DAY

SOMETHING FLASHY

"This costume was designed for Elton's first appearance at the Troubadour, which was his first appearance in America," explains Julian Day. "We sort of based it slightly on the real costume, but we took a little bit of licence with it."

In the previous scene, Elton chooses a pair of platform boots and tells his lyricist, "I need to make an impact, Bernie. It's all about being cool. It's just going to be me and a piano out there." At the Troubadour, Elton's platform boots almost steal the show. "These rather fabulous heels may be tricky to peddle a piano in, but they gave Elton the strength and confidence to give what is probably one of the most iconic inaugural performances ever," says Egerton.

Opposite Elton, before he discovers his passion for fashion.
Below "You'll look like a tit," Bernie tells Elton of his Troubadour dungarees and platform boots. Julian Day, *Rocketman*'s costume designer, disagrees.

BUSBY BERKELEY

"The *Honky Cat* costumes are used to show Elton's rise to fame, and the excess of money. It's a very Busby Berkeley outfit," explains Julian Day. The vision behind *Honky Cat* shows off separate sections that illustrate the burgeoning success and the growing notoriety, of Elton's wealth. "It's where Elton is really discovering his identity," says Egerton. "So Julian's design throughout the number has the looks growing in kind of fabulousness and colour and vibrancy, and it crescendos with this piece, and a big dance number. Which involves myself and Richard Madden having a little dance-off on top of a huge spinning record."

Below Supporting cast members ensure a comfortable landing.

Above The height of comfort and luxury – Elton and Reid lounge in style.

Above The "top hats" routine was not included in the final movie.

Below Elton and Reid have the time of their lives, in a deleted scene.

THE BIRD SUIT

For the majority of the film, Elton is surrounded by people who are suited and booted, very uptight, whereas he is this character, as the film progresses, who wears more and more flamboyant clothing to make him standout from all the muted colours.

"I love this costume. It's a serious contender for my favourite," says Egerton. "It's used at a point in the film, very cleverly placed by Julian, where Elton is beginning to have an acute sense that things aren't quite right, and that he isn't entirely fulfilled by his new-found success and fame."

The 'bird suit' costume, worn by Elton at the Royal Albert Hall show following a fight with John Reid, represents the absurdity of Elton's life. "When we shot this scene, all it said in the script was I enter on stage. And I found myself jumping in the air, flapping my wings like a funky chicken," reveals Egerton.

For Taron, this costume took a long time to fit: "We did many, many hours of fittings," the actor says. "Which can feel like quite a laborious process. But when you're working with someone like Julian, who is a genuine collaborator, as well as a brilliant creative, the time does pass quicker."

Opposite The "funky chicken".
Below The colourful bird suit disguised Elton's true unhappiness.

> "THIS COSTUME MADE MY BUM LOOK BIG. I'M BLESSED WITH
> JUNK IN THE TRUNK." TARON EGERTON

"MY FIRST THOUGHT WAS TO ACTUALLY MAKE SURE THAT ELTON WAS HAPPY WITH EVERYTHING, BECAUSE IT IS REPRESENTING HIS LIFE AND THE LAST THING I'D WANT TO DO WAS NOT REPRESENT HIM FULLY. WHEN HE CAME DOWN TO LOOK AT THE STUDIO AND LOOK AT THE SETS, I PRESENTED ALL THE CONCEPT DRAWINGS TO HIM, WHICH HE LOVED, IT WAS A BIG RELIEF. I THOUGHT IF ELTON LIKES THE CLOTHES, THEN THERE'S NOT MANY PEOPLE THAT CAN DISPUTE THAT."

JULIAN DAY

GOING UNDER

"This costume was designed for one of the appearances of Elton in Australia," begins Julian Day. "What he actually originally wore was a Louis XIV outfit, but I just felt that I wanted to do something that was slightly different, again, for our film. And I thought of Britain's most iconic characters…Queen Elizabeth I. We could have done some very nice period shoes, but I chose the very iconic Dr. Martens boots."

On set, Egerton was aware of the importance of the costume choice and its relevance to the scene, even if it meant feeling uncomfortable. "With a role like this, you have to succumb to the fact that the costumes aren't always going to be comfortable. But it's that sense of Elton's claustrophobia, that he's hemmed in, that

the clothes he's beginning to choose are about having an armour, protecting himself with increasingly large and thick costumes."

Indeed, it's during this particular concert in the movie that Elton makes some remarks on stage – and the costume had to juxtapose those comments. "I had this outrageous speech, in which Elton says some really quite crazy things [about religion] and pushes the line of what's deemed to be acceptable, really," says Egerton. "It's a very painful moment for Elton, but it's one where I think he's giving in to reckless abandon and self-destruction. But having this enormous, garish silhouette, allows you as an actor to kind of qualify the craziness of what he says."

Left Queen Elton I and John Reid backstage in a scene that was deleted.
Below and **Opposite** "My loyal subjects!"

> "ELTON IS A TRUE FASHION ICON. ELTON REALLY DOES HAVE HIS OWN STAMP AND IDENTITY, WHEN IT COMES TO NOT JUST HIS SOUND, BUT ALSO TO HIS VISUAL. NO ONE HAS EVER DONE IT LIKE HE HAS."
>
> JULIAN DAY

"IT WAS QUITE DAUNTING, THE IDEA OF REPRESENTING ELTON THROUGH HIS CLOTHING. HE'S KNOWN FOR HIS FABULOUS STAGE WEAR AND THE WEALTH OF THE CLOTHES. IT WAS A FABULOUS OPPORTUNITY, AND A SLIGHTLY DAUNTING OPPORTUNITY." JULIAN DAY

Above Costume Designer Julian Day with some of his creations.

Left A selection of colourful costumes.

Opposite Above Left Julian Day, Taron Egerton and the bird suit.

Opposite Above Right Taron in the Wizard of Oz costume.

Opposite Taron as Elton, with a selection of fantastic glasses.

Overleaf Elton John and Taron Egerton at the Elton John AIDS Foundation Academy Awards Viewing Party, February 24, 2019.

EAT ME. DRINK ME.

For the integral Wonderland scene, set in a New York gay bar, Julian Day's choice of costume had to be just right. "I felt absolutely that in the *Bennie and the Jets* sequence Taron needed to feel cool and feel sexy, because it's a very charged scene, it's a very drug fuelled scene, and it ends with Elton in a sort of fairly debauched situation... so there's also darkness to it, as well."

THE WIZARD OF OZ

Julian Day: "This outfit appears towards the end of the film, and it appears in a restaurant scene where Elton is having dinner with Bernie and his mother, and the song that it represents is *Goodbye Yellow Brick Road*. Dexter said, 'Look, you know, we're doing *Goodbye Yellow Brick Road*? Will you design something that has some relevance to that?' I thought of *The Wizard of Oz*. So, we've got the ruby red slippers, we've got the metal shirt from the Tin Man, the fur coat is the lion, the straw hat is for the scarecrow. So they all sort of represent something, and obviously there's a little emerald belt buckle there for the Emerald City. And Taron wore a little emerald earring...which he even got his ear pierced for!"